TRIUMPH HOUSE
Poetry with a Purpose

DAYS OF OUR LIVES

Edited by

Steve Twelvetree

First published in Great Britain in 2001 by
TRIUMPH HOUSE
Remus House,
Coltsfoot Drive,
Peterborough, PE2 9JX
Telephone (01733) 898102

HB ISBN 1 86161 931 6
SB ISBN 1 86161 936 7

FOREWORD

For many of us the medium of poetry offers us a voice - a voice to speak out and let others know what we feel, think and desire. It is this vital bridge of communication that lets us share our innermost thoughts and messages on life to people who may need that vital surge of poetic inspiration. It offers experience to those with none or little, spreads light to those in darkness and at the same time it encourages others that they are not alone.

Days Of Our Lives is a unique collection of poetry written in a variety of styles with the theme of 'I remember when'. The poems are easy to relate to and encouraging to read, offering engaging entertainment to their reader.

This delightful collection is sure to win your heart, making it a companion for life and perhaps even earning that favourite little spot upon your bookshelf.

Steve Twelvetree
Editor

Contents

THE HOUR IS VERY LATE

The hour is very late. It's important that we have truth.
The churches teach all sorts of rules. Of that I have ample proof.
Read the Word of God. The authorised version is best.
See what God Himself doth say and you'll be truly blessed.
He sent His Son to save us all from rejection, sin and shame.
Do you want precious liberty? Just call upon His Name.
The world has got in a terrible state, though God had made it so good
And many people in the world still bow to worship stone and wood.
Wake up! Wake up while there's still time. God is still on the throne.
Jesus will soon return to Earth, to gather up His own.
Don't leave it too late until we see Him coming in the sky.
Gaze above. Seek God's great love.
Call for His mercy. He'll hear your cry.

Winifred R Pettitt

Aunty Molly

I remember Molly
As an Aunty she was fun
Forever just one step ahead
Before others had begun

We played those endless games of draughts
(On Sunday quite a sin)
And though I didn't know it then
She always let me win!

She laughed at life and always had
An eye for the absurd
And every now and then she'd crack
And say a naughty word!

Sunday School picnic races
Were where she showed her best
Though easily the oldest
She soon outran the rest

She was interested in everything
Not afraid to share her views
No one better in the village
You could go to for the news!

So she lived her life with passion
Often laughter, then a tear
And though of humble station, yet
Of no one lived in fear

Yes, I miss my Aunty Molly
She was always lots of fun
And something tells me where she is
The laughter has begun.

John Bathgate

LOOKING BACK

I'm sure this is the spot
Where the old oak tree stood
It was here where the cows are grazing
Between the farm and wood

Here we would spend the summers
That flew on lightning wings
And that old hollow oak tree
Served as many things

Today perhaps a pirate ship
Battling through the gales
The highest branch a crow's-nest
And leaves were billowing sails

Tomorrow then a castle strong
That would never ever fall
Each branch would be a mighty gun
The hollow trunk the wall

And once it was a spaceship
That took us to the moon
No rocket ever flew so fast
To be there and back by noon

I'm sure that's where the old tree stood
Though many years have passed
It was there where the cows are grazing
When I played here last.

J Feaviour

The Old Jacket

(To my late Mum and Dad)

Dad's shabby old jacket still hangs behind the door,
It was his favourite, but alas he's not here anymore.
Snug and cosy, it fitted like a well-worn shoe,
Worn in the sheds, garden, and often the village too.

Destined for the dustbin Mother always threatened!
But Dad always retrieved it at the very last second.
Now my sad Mother touches it at least once a day,
It's the very last thing she wants to throw away.

John Mitchell

MEMORIES OF CHRISTMAS

Christmas was a magic time when I was young.
I retain and recall many memories

C is for *children* with *crackers* and *chocolates*
and *choirs* sweetly singing *Christmas carols.*
H is for *holly* with red berries clustering
holidays for children full of *happiness.*
R is for *reindeer,* we searched all the sky for
and the time for *religion,* the true meaning.
I is for *ice* so white that sparkled and crackled
and *ice cream* we had for a bounteous tea.
S is for *snow* with *snowballs,* and building *snowmen*
and *sledges* we loved to *scamper* downhill.
T is for *tree,* beautifully decorated
with trimmings and baubles, and flashing lights.
M is for *mistletoe* hanging down for kissing
and *music* always playing favourite tunes.
A is for *adults,* grown-ups celebrating
and for *apples* and oranges and all kinds of treats.
S is for *Santa* with *sacks* of toys, surprising
and for *songs* and *smiles* from everyone.

Terry Daley

The Forgotten Ones

In the cold, dark evening,
bewildered by the glittering lights,
the little girl stands in front of the pane of glass,
she hopes a miracle might happen.

Her nose touches the shop window,
(loaded with goods of the season).
Her eyes do not blink, but get misty
until crystal pearls roll down her cheeks,
she wipes them off with the back of her hand.

Her ragged dress barely covers her knees,
nothing warms her bare, blue feet.
The innocent child does not understand
why Christmas forgets some children,
everything is so close to her,
no distance lies in-between,

only the thickness of the glass.
So near, and yet . . . so far!

Victoria E Tejedor

DRIFTING

summer idling
reading
possibly praying
by an ocean

the laboured breathing of the surf upon the sand
its rasp along the shingle
its cough and splutter against the rocks
pluck at my attention
        like Grampa
        fading in the next room

sunny day
warm-sad reflections
carried off
on a turning tide

Stephen Eric Smyth

I Remember When

'Tis Christmas 1990, we're in a foreign land.
Our families are far away, but they all understand.
We're on the Saviour's errand, we're working for our King.
We know we will be happy and carols we will sing.

We're in our second childhood, we're looking for St Nick,
We search for Christmas gifts and cards, and open them real quick.
'Tis little Johnnie's drawing of Santa and his sleigh,
Little Susie's home-made star, we gaze at them and say -
'Oh, isn't he an artist, and Susie's such a pet.'
We love them all so very much, our folk we'll ne'er forget.

Now we must make our Christmas, we'll congregate today,
We'll share the food and all the fun, and silly games we'll play.
We'll tell each other stories of Christmases now gone.
We come from different cultures, traditions carried on.

Great Grandma's cookie-baking, and Grandpa's Santa hat.
We each have something good to tell, we'll sit around and chat.
The day has gone, the time well spent, we'll finish with a prayer
We'll thank our God for His dear Son, born in a stable bare.

Winifred Knell

INSTANT RECALL

Memories of other times,
Are drifting o'er my mind.
Memories of better days
And some that were unkind.

Holidays with those I've loved
And day trips here and there.
Those were oh, such happy times
A life without a care.

Jumping from an aeroplane.
The world beneath my feet.
Floating softly, down to Earth,
Thus made my day complete.

Walking through an autumn wood,
As leaves turn gold to brown.
Smiling at its majesty
And leafy eiderdown.

Grandma died and broke my heart.
Her memory lingers still.
Now and then a silent tear,
My heart, will overfill.

Cosy nights beside the fire.
The embers all aglow.
Looking out into the night
And praying 'twill go slow.

Memories are made of this.
Or so the songs all say.
I will hold them, in my mind,
From now 'til Judgement Day.

M J Plummer

Golden Band

Golden band around my finger,
Memories in my mind still linger,
Memories of a marriage band.
A simple wedding, nothing grand.
We made the choice and wed in May.
A few fond friends, a sunny day.
Our love we knew and love is rare,
And our lives we wished to share,
But life is not a gleaming roadway,
I went my way, he went his way
We shared our bodies, not our thoughts.
We had a marriage bond of sorts.
We made our promise to each other.
From then he was my only lover.
I feel sure I was his love dream.
We lost our way or so it seems.
Our love just died. It should have grown.
Now he's away and I'm alone.

J E Blissett

The Thought Of You

What have I got to do
Without your tenderly kiss
Day or night
When you walked away
Without saying goodbye.
Nobody will ever know
Why did you go?
I didn't do anything wrong
I thought our love would last forever
We had spent so much together.
What have I got to do
To feel your heart
Beating again close to mine?
My world has fallen apart
Without you in my life.
The thought of you
Always comes back
Your smile, rainbow of the sky
Made me feel alive
Now all my days are blue.

Paolo Debernardi

THE OLD MINE

I called at the old mine, still there, now silent like the grave,
Its housing stripped bare, stands with broken windows -
gaunt eyes that stare,
Old wire hangs from grimed walls as would angry knarled claws,
Here and there, an hobnailed boot, lamps and broken cups
strewn on the cobbled floor,
I dropped a stone down the shaft - a laugh - a distant splash,
The icy hand of fear laid heavily on the bone.
No more pit widows, left alone, to sit and stare, at the flames
that flicker,
In a coal-fired, pitch-black dampened grate.

Harry Glover

Looking Back To Smiters

Where is he that smote thee?
After all these years
Now Thou art ascended
He, without all the cheers;
How feels that hand
Thrust forth with strength
When Emmanuel came close
An arm's length.
Blindfolded, spat upon
Taunted, as if He could not see
Yet not as man, his pleasure
An answer would be.
Where is he that smote thee?
Did he learn what to do
When you prayed 'Father, forgive'
Did he ask forgiveness too?

Sarah Smeaton

THE WINDOW

You lean out of the pane, dark eyes on me,
your face so lovely, framed in longest hair.
What stranger future could you ever see?

Beyond the glass, a vision of might-be-free
with you and me to live and love and share.
You lean out of the window, dark eyes on me,

and smile and almost word a silent plea:
'Take me now, I'll come back, who knows where?'
What stranger future could you ever see

beyond the peal of bells, beyond the sea;
might my lips never kiss that furtive tear?
You lean out of the window, dark eyes on me,

forever and a day to disagree
with fate and cast aside all prudent care.
What stranger future could you ever see

in runes or sticks or antique stones' decree
or in the lashing ocean's wild despair?
You lean out of the window, dark eyes on me;
what stranger future could you ever see?

Francis Pettitt

MEMORIES

It seems like many moons
Have passed
All leaves merrily dance
As the windmill
Of my mind
Remember happy times
When we warmed
Our hands in the snow
And
The snowman smiled
As the sweet sun shines.

Helen Owen

OLDE MAGIC

I'll tell you a story, a story of 'olde'
Times of magic and pure solid gold
I can see us now, how happy we were
A home full of love and happiness there
Snow rides in the horse and cart
Days of yore that touched your heart
Jingle bells and 'Silent Night'
Fireside's glow that felt so right
Mistletoe, holly, fruit and pud
Those times did us the world of good
How beautiful the first snowflake
A glass of port, and Christmas cake
Coloured lights along the lane
Please, please take me there again
We're still happy, of course we are
All of us have come so far.
But I'd give the world if I could go
Back to those days of Christmas snow
To the days, the best we ever had
Living at home with Mam and Dad.

Lucy Lee

FEELING LIKE A SORE THUMB

Why is it I can't be outgoing
Whenever I'm asked to a 'do'?
My words don't seem to be flowing,
And I work myself into a stew.
Because I feel I'm a loner,
And don't have a man at my side,
Please don't think I'm a moaner . . .
I just can't go along with the tide.
When widowed you somehow feel surely
You're sticking out like a sore thumb.
Or could it be simply purely
Self pity? That makes anyone glum.
I sit here and find all around me
Are people, happy in pairs,
While I'm feeling lost and at sea
And I'm positive no one else cares!

E Balmain

O Love, For Delights

We walked together hand in hand
In the twilight of the evening
As I listened to the words of her mouth
They were sweet words
As sweet as flowers
That sent a sweet smell in the air
That filled my nostrils
Truly, this is my friend
I could not turn my eyes from her
Everyone that passed by
Looked at us
Her beauty was fair as the moon
And her smile was clear as the sun
When we embraced each other
My heart leapt like chariots in flight
Don't turn aside and walk away
Trembling to utter those soft words
I will hold your hand at all times
And when I remember that moment
My desire will still be toward you
Don't walk away I say!

Ebenezer Essuman

BRAINSTORM

I remember when - you smiled at me,
I remember losing - my liberty,
I remember too - my childhood,
I remember how - no one understood,
How came the day - when we were wed,
I remember my cramp - on our first night in bed,
I remember how we - forgot to book,
The honeymoon suite - in the 'Rookery Nook',
I remember wandering - up and down the street,
Begging lodging - from any we should meet,
I remember how down - the rain ran,
Down on the roof - of the camper van,
I remember the time - our bairn was born,
I remember my drinking - until the early morn,
I remember most - most every night,
How I shared a bed with you - oh what a sight,
I recall the neighbours calling you 'Droopy Drawers',
I have difficulty recalling - being on all fours,
I will always remember you - until the day that I die,
But what I cannot remember - is *why?*

John L Wright

Everybody Loved Saturday Night

Jiving was banned at the Palais de Danse
It would look out of place in that shrine to romance
So I went instead to the Cricket Club hop
An event which was known as the Bignall End bop
I twisted and turned in a skirt of red felt
Secured at the waist by a broad waspy belt
My petticoats twirled ever higher and higher
As I spun to the beat of 'Great Balls of Fire'
Elvis's 'Don't' played at ten fifty-five
Three minutes before the bus would arrive
A two-minute smooch then a one-minute run
So ended our fifties-style Saturday fun.

Margaret Butler

CRIBBAGE

The chill
From the window
Some time ago
Now
Although
The friendly face
As he dealt the cards
Studied them
Intently
If but for a second or two
Put down two
For the crib
Waited patiently
Whilst I dithered and dickered
Smiled as I made my choice
For the crib
Advancing as we took our turns his peg a few places
Announcing after that next time it would be my crib
If that happened to explain anything
Or everything
His trained eye knew
What to throw away
And what to keep
Whilst now if I am left with this memory
To decide by
If today I make my choice more rapidly
In some things if not in others.

C J Bayless

I Remember When . . .

I remember when . . . the streets were safe to walk.
A friendly Bobby on the beat would stay a while and talk.
I remember when . . . the streets were safe to play,
The children wandered far away, but came home safe again.
There were no muggers on the streets, no vandalism then.
I remember when . . murders and drugs and drunks,
And yobbo gangs and car pursuits, we heard of very few.
Our young were taught through discipline, as we were taught before.
A hundred lines we got in class; *'I must talk no more.'*
I remember when . . . our doors were left unlocked,
Our windows open wide and free.
We had no uninvited guests to rob us and then flee.
Oh! For the days of not long ago, I hope they'll soon return,
Of morals, love, and loyalty, and respect for which we yearn.
If I am living at that time, my grateful praise I'll sing
Unto the Lord, who promised us the best of everything.

Barbara Wait

Reflections Of You

Three sisters: one of them, my mother
Died, leaving me watching her spirit
Living in the others.
Glimpses, now and then
At their faces,
Bring you back to me
In a shadowy reflection
Which leaves me numb
Because I know you are gone.
I can't really touch you
Or reach you through them.
They are a remembrance,
A memorial to your soul.
When their faces disappear
Into the night
And three souls
Become one again,
As they were in the beginning,
I will hold the memory
In my head; for their monuments to you
Will be fallen.

An empty room
Contains the silence
Of a voice, lost forever.
Only repeated, over and over,
The same words on a tape recorder.
Phrases caught in time
Representing the day you spoke them.
The magnetic-tape voice
Can never answer my questions.

Debbie Perks

The Artist

Life's canvas challenges the artist
To take the first stroke, with paints
Of sorrow and turmoil.
His palette provides a colour of rage
And anger, as the brush boldly
Creates the upturned bottle,
From which the fiery liquid escapes.
As it fills the canvas so it fills
His soul which screams at memories
He tries to forget.
Standing back the artist recalls
Innocent years and the brush
Slowly, silently paints a youthful reminder.
Smiles of joy fill the artist's face
But the brush strokes tell a different story.
The toy is battered and bruised,
Cracked like the artist's inner shell.
Penetrating pain devours him as he
Loses all control and the brush once
More paints the Devil's fire, as it
Breathes onto the canvas.
Colours of blue fill his palette as
He paints with sadness and solitude.
As he lays his brush to rest,
He stares beyond the canvas,
Wondering what colours will
Fill the empty palette below.

Julie Broxton

So Very Happy

I am happy so very happy
I have told you before
When you go out of the door
I am happy so very happy
When you come back saying I am so cute
In my high-heeled boots.

I am happy so very happy
When you are back in the room
Holding those flowers in bloom
As you are spending more time
In our bedroom.

I am happy so very happy
When you start getting undressed
For another night's rest
I am happy so very happy
For you will not sleep yet
Yes, I bet I bet.

Keith L Powell

Christmas Memories

All little girls remind me of the Christmases we knew,
The excitement shared on Christmas morn was there for me and you.
We hardly slept the night before and couldn't wait to see
How many presents were in our sacks and what the gifts would be.
In the early hours we'd be awake and giggling and talking lay
Longing for the changing sky and to see the break of day.
We couldn't wait, so out of bed both of us would get,
Until a voice we knew and loved would say 'Oh no, not yet!'
And then dear Mum would change her tone 'You can open
just two each'
So in the sacks we'd rummage to see if we could reach
The presents we were hoping for, our lists were written with care.
Some things for ourselves and some games for us to share.
Such happy moments we have known together all the way.
Our lives have always been entwined and even to this day.
We're always joined in Christmas love and Christmas wishes
by the score.
There can't be sisters anywhere who love each other more.

Barbara King

A Precious Gift

The torment I received at school, from kids and staff alike,
Was not very Christian for a Catholic place in spite
Of all the 'preaching' of, 'God loves everyone,'
No matter who or what we are, or where we may come from.
But one special lady stood apart from all the rest,
Her kindness and her love and friendship, I remember best.
In winter she would always find a coat and boots for me,
In a plain and simple act of pure, sweet, charity.
I should have been a mean and bitter person now,
Affected by the cruelty of that low and unkind crowd.
But this dear lady showed a gentleness so great
I learned to love, like her, and not to hate.
I know her influence has always stayed with me,
And so I'd like to thank her for my own serenity.

S M Brown

'Twas Great To Be A Fifties Child

When coal fire smoke through frosty air
Would rise up straight to smudge the moon,
And when the bedroom windows bare,
Were icy in the afternoon,
And when the snow swirled through my sleep
To greet the crispest morning, piled
In alps around the garden, deep
'Twas great to be a Fifties child:

When steam trains puffed into the fog
Of pea soup dank Novembers past,
I'd love the smell of smoke and smog,
And then to hear the parting blast
Of steam which seared my soul and ears
And drove my brittle senses wild:
And made me think in later years
'Twas great to be a Fifties child:

When walks to school, with joy were graced
'Twas simple pleasures I recall,
Tall whelming elms, and twigs enlaced
With fragile webs embracing all:
When starry nights were still and calm
And on the moon a visage smiled,
I'm glad that I enjoyed such charm;
'Twas great to be a Fifties child.

Nicholas Winn

My Childhood

My childhood was so happy
Until I was just four,
We lived in a lovely wee cottage
And our grandparents lived next door.
We lived in a really small village
In Ireland, called Stradbally,
Where we had so many cousins
And lots and lots of family.
We were quite poor but very happy
It was a safe and lovely place to stay
But sadly due to unemployment
We were forced to move away.
So we left our wee rented cottage
To sail off to a foreign land
I cried all the way to Glasgow
I was too young to understand.
I hated life in a city
We had nowhere nice to play
Every holiday we went back to Ireland
And I always cried to stay.
There were no relatives at all here
Just the wee unit of our family
Although I made pals when I went to school
It never felt the same to me.
It was not until I was an adult
When I married and settled down
That I felt a part of Glasgow
Not just a foreigner from a wee Irish town.

Mary Anne Scott

THE HOLES IN YOUR SHOE

Cast your mind back,
To when we were kids,
Ration books, coupons,
Castor milk in tins, with rusty lids,

Soldiers return to pick up their lives,
In the land fit for heroes,
Scarred landscapes, towns full of rubble,
Gas mantles and crystal radios,

But the spirit that saw us through,
Soon was on the wane,
As reality hit home,
And nothing could ease their pain.

Life slowly returned to normal,
But what was normal after what they had been through?
Thrupence would buy a big bag of chips,
Cardboard cut-outs covered the holes in your shoe,

Debs and Teds brought a certain colour,
To those drab early fifties times,
Vera Lynn and Ann Shelton sang to packed houses,
But 'Rock Around The Clock' was rolling down the line.

When somebody down the street,
A television set first bought,
And hundreds of kids and some adults
A glimmer from outside through the hazy windows sought,

When Winston still gave his famous sign,
When Charlie Brown was born, and Al Jolson died,
Little Mo Connolly won the Grand Slam at Wimbledon,
Held that shiny shield aloft then broke down and cried,

Yes, I remember it as if it were only yesterday,
When poor King George died and Queen Elizabeth
came to stay.

P J Littlefield

THE DEAREST OF ALL

Remember in the Thirties
  how our family used to cope
With my father being ill at times
  Mother never had much scope.

She had to take on jobs of work
  for her budget to work out
I don't know how she managed this
  but we never went without

She was skilled in using a sewing machine
  and saved money through this chore
As she fashioned all the clothing
  that most of our family wore

She could paint and also decorate
  and did jobs for all the neighbours
And so the family life progressed
  from Mother's fruitful labours

We were a large mixed family
  six sisters and four brothers
Our parents were both Christian souls
  but at the forefront was my mother

She was the saviour of our family
  with Father being ill
We shall never forget the debt we owe
  I don't think we ever will.

Lachlan Taylor

PRIMARY SCHOOL

Days that danced with golden light
Flaxen dust that streamed from windows high
The salty striking smell of plasticine
And the way the colours merged to leave a
kind of browny-green.

Dressing up in high-heeled shoes
And Mum's new beads that she happened to lose
Bringing in that pine cone for show and
The way your heart jumped when you heard the bell.

Scraping your knee on the playground floor
Picking at the scab while the register's called
Listening to stories that take you away
Then you're dropped back to Earth at the end of the day.

Rhiannon Moore (15)

CRICKET

I was saying yesterday
That we came out one summer's day
To play
In May,
Or thereabouts.

Nicola Barnes

A Soldier's Christmas

The battlefield lay in its silence
As somewhere in the distance far away
A lonely piper played seasonal carols
And my thoughts wandered home to Christmas Day.

The turkey would now be served and ready
Plum pudding with a sixpence inside
Laughter would ring around the table
And my brother would sit with his new bride

The coal fire would warm even the coldest
And Dad would sit with pride as he watched
Our smiles as from the eldest to the youngest
We all began to empty our woollen sock

An apple down the toe or even an orange
Some toffees and if the rations would permit
Maybe a few gilded chocolates
With peanuts and walnuts if they would fit

We each had a present from dear Santa
I know that it didn't amount to a lot
A pair of socks or gloves that Mom had knitted
Or some hankies, were all we ever got

But the love of my mother was all we needed
And a sip of Grandad's beer for a treat
We would play some games and then carol singing
And all agree, this Christmas was hard to beat

This time tomorrow Christmas will be over
The guns will pound and kill without regret
But just for now I'll listen to the piper
And pretend that I am home where dreams are kept.

Gillian Mullett

WHERE ARE WE NOW?

Where are they now - those golden days
Of cold clean air and water pure,
Unblemished skies, no holes or tears,
No satellites, just moon and stars.
When poppies, cowslips, daisies dressed
Green fields in brightly-patterned garb.
Thatched cottages, Shire horses ploughed,
From corn sheaves stooks to haystacks laid?

Where are they now - those childhood days
Of golliwogs and teddy bears,
Dolls and tea sets, hopscotch, skipping,
Hoops, Meccano, yo-yos spinning.
Painted forts from boxes fashioned.
Tadpoles, catapults and marbles,
Snakes and ladders, snap and patience
Happy families - fun and frolic?

Where are they now - those wartime years
Ration books and empty larders.
Children parted from their loved ones,
Sirens warning, air raid shelters.
Towns and cities bombed in ruins.
Maimed and dead, such grief and horror.
People's spirit, pride and courage
Helped rebuild their lives from nothing?

Where are they now - those memories
Of family, friends and years gone by,
Faded now but still recalling
Changing places, lifestyle, people,
Vague dreams lost in time that passes.
Now we've seen our children growing
From the past to present, future.
They are here now - where are we now?

Pauline Phillips

Lost Love!

I knew not love ere first we met,
My life was planned, emotions set.
One glimpse of you, your comely face,
My heart was filled with loving grace!

We kissed, we loved, you took my name,
We played in full, life's fleeting game.
Till one sad day, no parting word,
You slipped away, your voice unheard!

I live on still, my love has gone,
I search for strength to carry on,
Till one sweet day again we meet,
My life, at last, will be complete!

A E Garrod

A Special Place

There is a special place, where we used to walk
If only now I could see her face
To be with her, to see her, and to hear her talk
To go back once more to that special place.

This place was by the riverside
Where we would sit and have a snack
Gazing upon the river, so far, so wide
If only those days would come back.

We could see the horizon all around
Between the spires and chimneys in the town
See also the south, the west and the east
A panoramic view, so lucky to gaze upon such a feast.

We looked on the river, both north and south
A fleeting glimpse of the seal, and then he was gone
Leaving the geese, the yachts, and the peaceful scene
To feel the salty tang upon the mouth.

The sky was blue, but the east wind was cruel
We were well wrapped up, we had been there before
Over the way we heard the children at school
As they stopped for lunch, tumbling through the door.

It was time to go, home for lunch
Meeting friends on the way we would stop and chat
Time meant nothing, we had been in our world
Even loath to leave it, for that warm, comfy flat

I remember it clearly, the red faces, the windswept hair
How I wish that we were there
Now she has gone from that very special place
I go back, and look in the sky, for that lovely, happy face.

K R French

My Mother

Watching her, green-fingered in the garden,
Old and gnarled but yet unbowed,
I recall her as she was,
So young and vibrant,
Lithe and golden in the sun,
My world, my everything.
I see her scooping water from the spring
In summer's drowsy noontide;
Bright diamonds dripping from the pitcher's lip,
To sparkle in the velvet moss
And on her freckled feet.
I feel her warmth, her pillowed softness
As, tucked behind her in the chair,
She'd tell me tales of wonder and delight
That sped me wide-eyed,
Off to Fairyland.
And I remember too, her sheltering slightness,
Cradled close across her precious brood,
Throughout the warning sirens wailing
And that fearful
Raining down of death.
And even now, for me today,
With love and wisdom, still she stands,
A rock in every time of trouble.
The first and dearest blessing of my life.

Jean Oxley

MEMORY OF FIRST DAY IN SCHOOL

I started my first day in school,
In 1962,
England was strange to me,
You see,
For I was shy, I was alone,
Africa at one time was my home,
The new school was mixed,
During playtime,
A tall girl had her eyes on me
fixed,
She walked up to me,
In the playground,
Like a wolf she came to hound,
We were both Asians of one kind,
And is this the only friend,
I could find?

I was scared and did not speak,
To that, she picked up her right feet,
To give me a kick,
I had to act quickly,
I grabbed hold of her flying leg,
Before it got to my chin,
I could not let her win,
So I gave it a good pull,
As she slid falling backward,
On the hard floor,
And got up feeling like a big fool,
After that,
I was the favourite in the school.

A Bhambra

AFTER YULETIDE

It's just after Yuletide
But the smell of stale cooking lingers
And won't easily hide
After the burnt roast cinders

Air freshener and atomisers
Still don't hide the odour
Of harmonisers
Baking and stale flour

Leftover food
Jellies and cakes
Soaps and bath salts looking good
Christmas cake and home bakes

Leftovers in freezer bags
Everything covered over with tinfoil
Must go and relax in aromatherapy oil
And put on my glad rags.

Ann Copland

BRIEF ENCOUNTER

My father: slower now, grey-haired -
Stooped and seventy - retains the
Body of an active man. Hands
Still powerful are now impaired -
A tremor frustrates delicate
Work. He watches as I set
The ladder right and climb stiff-legged
To reach the sill. First I locate
A place to grip, then clean the pane.
My tentative reach with soapy
Sponge, cack-handed smear with squeegee,
From other men would bring disdain -
'Let's have a go, I know the game,'
Is all he says. Scorning my tools
(Set in his ways) he fetches
Chamois and scrim, the very same
That in the past have seen millions
Of windows pristine clean. Leaded
Or shop glass: all the same to him;
Bays and bows, fanlight or mullion
He has cleaned. Ignoring feeble
Protests he swarms the ladder with
A practised tread . . . years slip away
With every step. Transformed: muscle
Memory conjures up this younger
Man, still working at his peak, as
He'd been when I was just a lad.
Balancing and stretching, further
He sways, reaching to the window's
Distant edge. Rhythm and power;
Economy in every stroke,
This craftsmanship admired below.
Ten feet above my head I watch
His flow: balance, grace, confidence -
Decisiveness in every stroke -

Sureness of touch I could not match.
And I am grateful when he's through
For cleanliness of glass - a job
Well done - and sharing with me
This hidden younger man I knew.

Patrick Osada

Travelling The Years Down Memory Lane

Into my 92nd year, I look back and treasure,
The many memories, most of which give me pleasure.
The First World War, four years of misery and strife,
As one very young, wondering what lay ahead in life.

Summer holidays at seaside were such good fun,
The weather always seemed fine, with plenty of sun,
Building sandcastles, paddling, watching puppet show,
Wishing days were longer, when to bed I had to go.

My childhood was happy, no expensive gifts like today,
Special treat, the cinema's Saturday afternoon matinee,
We enjoyed simple pleasures, at little cost,
That is now something of which the art has been lost.

Going to famous Wembley Exhibition, seeing wonderful displays,
From Oriental countries, learning their culture and unusual ways,
The Second World War, long years of deprivation,
Blackout, sounding sirens, bomb blast and devastation.

Setting up in business, and after a shaky start,
Finding success, glad we didn't lose heart.
Celebrating my husband's birthday every 25th of December,
Cosy Christmas parties with family get-together.

Watching my son receive his Doctor of Philosophy degree,
After studying at Cambridge and Leicester University.
His happy marriage and two children sweet.
The pleasures we shared, making our joy complete.

Annual holidays, travelling in every direction,
Each year pastures new, our ultimate destination,
To the coast we came, our retirement to share,
Halcyon days followed, all being 'set fair'.

Now I'm alone, but nothing will ever steal
Past happy memories, and their magic appeal.

E K Jones

YEARS OF CHILDHOOD

The world around in torment lay -
For us, it was a summer's day.
We were too young to understand
The perils that beset our land.
Too old, too young, my nearest kin
Who saw four years of war begin.
Its grimmest horrors passed us by,
How fortunate, my friends and I!
No radios, no cold TV
Shattered our childish peace; to see
A trainload pass of waving 'boys',
New young recruits whose cheerful noise
Hid ignorance but little less
Than ours, taught us no bitterness.
Our parents guarded us from fear,
We hardly knew when death was near.
One single night the bombs rained down
And cruelly hit our ancient town.
But still in sturdy strength we grew,
And tragedies we scarcely knew.
We too rejoiced when warring ceased,
Such optimism was released.
It seems to me, two worlds we spanned;
Though few things went as they were planned,
And harsh the times in which we grew,
Such early years I'd wish for you.
That precious seven gave to me
A core that brought stability.
However little, it's deserved
I'll pray its strength may be preserved.

Kathleen M Hatton

What Went Wrong?

I remember when
Bedtimes were before ten
Hide and seek, making a den
Scribbling everywhere with a pen.

I remember when
I used to skive off school.
Do anything to break that rule
God, I was such a fool!

I remember when
My brother and I
Used to fight
Argue both day and night

I remember when
Mum and Dad were together
One of the happiest times ever

I remember when
I started experiencing life
Something I never got right.

Memories made
I don't want to know
Except my daughter,
I love her so

But something I know by what I've done
Think about what you do before it's done

So now to concentrate on the future,

My family I've got I long to keep
My partner, my daughter, my son.
We're going to have loads of fun.

And I'll teach them never to do what I have done
And let our love drift on and on
Till life has ended a happy one.

Michelle Barnes

Inglorious War

Exhausted and cold throughout,
My comrades and I.
Tired by hacking coughs,
The gateway to peace is locked.

Staggering to safety,
Withdrawing from the battle.
Shouting, screeching
Death is upon us.

Trying to escape the bloodshed,
Wounded and hardly able to move
Venturing towards the gateway,
I hold no hope.

A thick gas emerges in the air,
'Gas!' somebody bellows, 'masks on.'
A man screams,
Too late.

A soldier staggers towards me,
Gas rapidly filling his lungs,
Blood spreads over his face like water on paper,
He chokes as he drowns in his blood and mucus.

I never imagined the horror
Of experiencing the death throes of
Dying comrades, their pain and agony
As blood is expelled from bursting lungs.

The image of soldiers
Blurred in the thick clouds,
Phantasmagoric, spectral,
Indelibly imprinted on my mind.

Mutilated, mangled bodies,
Piled ungainly upon a cart,
Soon to be laid in Mother Earth,
Buried but never forgotten.

I am left with the conclusion,
There is no glory in sacrificing
One's life for one's country,
Only pain, despair and oblivion.

Natalie Ward (13)

WINTER NOCTURNE, BOSCOMBE CLIFFS

Midwinter was enough to bring
The ghosts of those I had desired,
But moonlight's muted offering
Made music too, and so inspired

Love's dormant rhapsody in me,
That as with gilded thread she cast
Her planished pathway through the sea,
I felt the flame of visions past.

The lights from some far-distant shore,
Like dancing stardust, seemed to play
Across the memory and restore
The rapture of a summer's day.

And faces born of vanished dreams
In sylvan landscapes gathered there,
Still smiling by translucent streams
The waning seasons had laid bare.

The keening of the night wind stirred
My yearning for those far-off days,
And rhapsodised a song first heard
In half-forgotten woodland ways.

Perhaps it was not strange that such
An introverted sepia scene
Should move my bleeding heart to touch
Those phantom joys where youth had been.

For darkness trains the inner eye
To see what is no longer there,
And in the mind old ghosts drift by
To tell how things transpired - and where.

S H Smith

The Source

I looked for happiness and peace of mind
In being gentle, and in doing good;
But my reward was bitter tears at flood,
Unleashed by those to whom I was most kind.

I then imagined I would surely find
A strong and healthy body if I stood
In quiet solitude of field and wood,
Where ever-vital sun, life-giving, shined.

And I was wrong!
            But in the Word of God,
Within the pages of His Holy Book,
I found rich treasure and abounding wealth;
Along the path that Jesus Christ once trod,
Along the Way that He, unswerving, took,
Are peace of mind, and harmony, and health.

Dan Pugh

Goodbye

Now my wings have
Been broken
Now my life's been shattered
Now my world has been shaken
Myself has been battered
Pulled the strings from my mandolin
You have torn out my heart
All the trust thrown in the bin
You came and tore me apart
Turned my bright, to black
Told me, thousands of lies
You made my heart crack
Now I am saying goodbye
You can get on the train
4000 tears I have cried
Now I'm saying goodbye, no more pain
I'm angry I've now closed the door
Hurt me again, you will never
I've been the fool too damn long
I'm angry, angry, angry
All you ever did to me was wrong
You don't mean well, so leave me
Be . . .
You know what, you put me down
That isn't good for me
Now I just want out
You were never around
Now I'm very p****d and very angry
Wherever you go, you will have a shadow
Could you ever be free?
Now I'm just letting you go
Now . . . I'm saying goodbye
Must be a better door to open
And my wings would fly again

They shall fly
Don't want to see you again
Now I'm saying my goodbyes
You sure had me licked
Forever a constant sigh
Like a bad habit, it's you I have kicked
You sucked out all my sunshine
Left my days grey
Now I have got out in time
Found a better way.

D Riches

An Old Soldier

He sits all alone, every day, on the park bench,
His world in a tattered old bag,
If you had the time, he would show you his medals,
Wrapped up in the Union Jack.

When he was a young man he fought for his country,
On battlefields in far-off lands,
In trenches, in ditches, on wide barren deserts,
On hillsides, deep mud and hot sands.

Hand-to-hand fighting, no guns, for the bullets,
Water and food had all gone,
But pride in his homeland, the thought of his loved ones,
Gave him the will to fight on.

Returning to Blighty, they gave such a welcome,
Cheered him, 'Our Hero', they cried,
Presented his medals, for 'Outstanding Courage',
Carried him through the streets, shoulder high.

The years have rolled by, the battle's forgotten,
Today's generation pass by,
They laugh and they mock at this shabby old soldier,
For them, he was willing to die!

Jim Sargant

School Bully

I well remember when, young, harsh and cruel
You made my life a misery at school.
Your boldness taunted my timidity
And it was your delight to frighten me.
Pinches and punches - surreptitious kicks -
Blows from your little armoury of sticks -
These all combined to fill my days with fears
And brought me often to unhappy tears.
'Cry baby' you would shriek, your triumph won -
My misery was your idea of fun.
I brought a ball to school with me one day.
You seized it from me, and flung it away.
You tossed my hat onto a passing car
And jeered at my distress: I think there are
Few youthful situations much more sad
Than all the wretched torment that I had
At your hands to endure: you spoiled for me
The beauty of my childhood memory.

And yet, when I saw you the other day,
Your breath laborious, your face grown grey
With pain: the tell-tale hint of creeping blue
Around your lips, informing me that you
Are sick of heart, and fighting to survive
Until they do that bypass - keep alive
Somehow, struggle slowly on
Living - suddenly it had gone -
All the old bitterness. I can forgive
You: and I hope that we may live
In peace at last. Forget all aged wrong.
You are the weak one now, and I the strong.

Elsie Balme

Beaurepaire

What have they done to you, sad house?
Painted your face a scandalous white and blue.
- plaintive house.
Stripped the ivy from your walls
And let the porchway go to ruin where the odd tile falls.
No longer the red may spreads its fingers, by the
wrought iron gate.
No more the cherry's blossoms fall to the ground
When April is gone late.
Where is the plum tree, or the fuchsias - the roses on the lawn?
Were the apple trees burnt, or chopped up
When from the garden they were torn?

They've built some ghastly houses, in the garden where we
used to play,
In what was then the shady greenery of a better day.
What have you done - miserable people
To the place I used to live?
What is left of 'Beaurepaire' now?
What can it say, what can it give?

Jane Mills

Christmas Past

Oh, what joy filled my heart
When a child, thinking of Christmas
Snow so high before Christmas
That I had trouble to walk to school
Yet, so enjoyed the snowballing with my many friends
And the jolly snowman in the garden
With his coal-black eyes and nose
His mouth was made to
Smile, by a piece of thick wood
The snow was so soft it soon
Gave way to make my snowman grin
My father made my brother and me
A sledge big enough for six
Children to ride with constant laughing
We all would pull and push the sledge
Up the West Common hill to beyond West Parade, Lincoln
My brother would hold the sledge from slipping
Downhill, my four friends would board
My brother would sit as driver holding the rope reins
To steer the sledge, I would sit at the back to
Slow down the sledge on command
From my brother, after a jolly
Ride downhill, where the snow was very thick
The Brayford Basin at Lincoln
Froze over every year to 6" deep
On Friday nights for six weeks
A dance band played on the wharf side
Potatoes and chestnut vendors gave us hot food
Black large barrels had wood stakes of fire burners
And the dancers would waltz and fox-trot with heavenly delight
Oh! What wonderful happy days, when a child was
Young enough to be still a little child.

Alma Montgomery Frank

I Remember

I remember a time sitting on some rocks
And a waterfall cascading down
The water so clear as it formed a pool
To lap around my feet on the ground
The air so still and calm as the birds sang in the trees
With blue sky everywhere and warm sun upon my knees.
I remember the bridge and embankment where my cousins
would eagerly wait
For our car to appear on the lane
And Aunty waiting to greet us with tea and home-made cake.
I remember my nine and tied sitting patiently in their armchairs
Giving us hugs and kisses wrapping us in her bosom
happy to see us there.
A month at a time we stayed with them.
We played in the sun every day.
But Sundays were quite different
No outdoor games were allowed
Everyone went to Chapel Sunday morning prompt
Dressed in their Sunday best hat, gloves and shoes
And Bibles carried by most, quiet-spoken folk.
After the morning service parents took us home
Walking alongside the river seeing the swans glide along.
As soon as we reached the farmhouse the Bible put on the shelf
Our hat, gloves and shoes put away
A pinny wrapped around us worn for the rest of the day.
These are just a few of the things remembered
As I look back to my childhood holidays
With grandparents, cousins, farm animals
And the fun riding round on the carthorse
As we buried ourselves in the hay.

Barbara Boon

I Remember

I remember Grandpa old man
Weary and worn resting in the cornfield
As reapers harvested the corn
I remember Grandma, her long black skirt
Did flow as she cooked apple pie
For supper, on the hearth fire
All those years ago.
I remember her quote the Bible
Verse after verse from memory
A kind Godly woman
Leaving a spiritual legacy.

I remember Grandma washing clothes
In a big, round wooden tub
I can still hear the mangle screeching
The handle I turned at will.
I remember the great beech tree
That grew near the farmhouse door.
There we played as children
Toys we didn't own, still happy, contented
Sweet biscuits then were a treat
Many a time shoes were in holes
'Twas little covered our feet
Looking back on sweet memories
These modern ways I don't understand
One day I'll see Grandpa and Grandma again,
Perhaps in a cabin in the corner of
Glory Land.

Frances Gibson

WHEN SOMEBODY GOES . . .

It's a lonely feeling,
That's crept inside me,
Silently, but I can feel it.
They've gone,
A perfect person,
Gone.
Silently, innocently,
They've left our world.
They've gone to a new place,
A peaceful place,
Where I hope they'll be happy.
Remaining in our hearts,
With us, waiting for their return,
Yet knowing that they will never come back,
Because they've found heaven.
They've found a perfect place,
For such a perfect person.

Katie Burt

TAKEN FOR GRANTED

I remember taking you for granted when I was young,
Now that I am older, how I wish I had not done, Mum.
When I got married you telephoned me every week,
Lonely, how you craved conversation and you loved to speak.

I remember when I was little, I would laugh at you,
Now I'm mature, I can see this was a stupid thing to do.
Over the last few years, we went out on several trips,
Using buses and trains but you would never go on ships.

Although you were in intense pain, thought you would outlive me,
But in the schemes of life and death this was never to be.
I remember when we collected berries from the hedgerow,
You slipped and fell but then climbed up and had another go.

S Mullinger

THE WRITING ON THE CARDS

This is the day you wrote
Your Christmas cards,
Opened the cardboard box
With the red Robin on the top.

This is when you read your list,
Written in fine blue ink,
Your pen crossing off
Auntie Helen, adding the
Name of your consultant.

This is when you wrote
Each card, added a few words
Sent your love in an envelope
To your list of friends.

Now I lift the Robin,
Steal myself to look inside
Add your names to mine.

I put back the lid -
And notice Robin
Has salt tears on his breast.

Janet M Baird

EASTER TRAIL

Easter Time!
With Easter-trails,
from each bedroom
and down the stairs

Laid when youngsters
fast asleep -
round the house
we used to creep.

Paper slips
with written clue
to lead them to
a choc or two.

Mini-eggs with
various sweets -
little toys for
Easter treats.

Happy Days
in simple times -
Easter clues
in written rhyme.

Children's voices
echoing -
my thoughts of Love
Remembering!

Mary Skelton

A Village Boy

A Wiltshire village, truly a rural treasure
Looking back brings most pleasure
Playing by the river, or nearby copse
Biking to visit the two village shops

My infant school just next door
No chance of skiving school anymore
The milk warmed around a big open fire
Twenty-five village kids who sang like a choir

We did enjoy the country dancing
Some of us like elephants prancing
Skipping 'round the Maypole at the village fete
The highlight of the social calendar date

I never passed the 'Eleven Plus'
So twenty miles on the big school bus
Eight am, all us big kids would wait
Hoping that the school bus may be late

From 25 to 900, I thought I would get lost
I took sarnies in my Oxo tin to save the cost
On cross-country days I took a sickie
Mother agreed, no need to run when it was
hot and sticky

To get pocket money I had to earn my pay
Picking peas, sixpence a bushel, or loading hay
I was proud of my new bike with gears
Delivering my Echo's when I was twelve years

In the early days of a country lad
Sometimes hard but happy and glad
The fifties, good years for true country folk
Enjoying the pleasures unlike those from
the 'big smoke'.

Then the yuppies, townies and snobs moved in
A village community gone. What a sin!

John Babey

I REMEMBER AIR-RAIDS IN LONDON BLITZ

Sirens wailing full blast nigh every night,
Rushing down into Anderson by dimmed torchlight,
Comfortless, on slatted bunks 'til sound of all-clear,
While single bombs whistled, groups whooshed causing fear,
Thro' experience could gauge where one may explode,
Bunch of bombs falling vicious grapevine overload.

Outside the shelter, searchlights panning sky,
Floodlighting Luftwaffe trespassing our shut-eye,
Ack-ack volleys firing from nearby battery,
Hun pilots high, out of range, for sanctuary,
Heading for targets, if attacked bombed anywhere,
Limping back to base in Europe for fast repair.

Sometimes, before raids heard RAF overhead,
Gathered to shout good luck in Germany's hotbed,
The Earth trembled from our squadron's moaning low drone,
Heavily bomb-pregnant flew with constant groan,
On return, if clear sky tried to count our boys home,
If one missing screamed delight to spot last home, roam.

Roughly knew the time when foe would take flight
Luftwaffe departed our skies before dawn's light,
Thankfully, the all-clear would cheerfully sound,
We clambered from musty shelter indoor bound,
Jumped into freezing beds for remainder of kip,
Alive but aware others were dead from Hun's blitz.

We kept chickens who squawked all raid in fright,
Fewer precious eggs to collect after bad night,
But staunchly two ducks did not miss their large gifts laid,
Daily awaiting us despite daunting raid.
Relied upon them to conserve our small rations,
Beloved; admired their grit and resolute passion.

Hilary Jill Robson

The Button Box

As I ponder and finger each button with care,
Each one with a story cut from clothes now bare,
What a simple collection that fills the mind,
With memories so fragrant and tales so refined

Red brown and green, orange purple and blue
Square ones and round, oval and anchors too,
Every conceivable shape, colour and kind,
Except what I want now - I never can find.

A box full of buttons each one with a tale,
Of days long gone, when just a girl,
A dress mother made of a greenish hue,
Which fastened down front, with these buttons of blue.

These larger buttons all symmetrical and brown,
Were sewn on a coat when I first went to town,
Feeling important I strutted about,
In the 'A' line fashion I wanted to shout.

Oh these sparkling buttons came with a skirt,
To go with it I adapted a shirt,
To dances I'd go and feel really grand
The lights shining on them as I twirled around.

Now when I open the box it's to play with the young,
Colours and numbers and sizes what fun!
With grandchildren round me a simple game,
Will they always remember me by name?

Barbara Kirner

A Portrait Of Emily Kate

A silver frame sits on my mantle shelf.
Within this frame, a portrait of yourself.
You then, a dark-eyed beauty, so petite,
Smartly, exquisitely dressed, and oh so neat.
Full flush of youth, and soon to be a bride,
But fate decreed such sadness, for besides
Your husband of a short span, dying while at war,
Your only child, a baby son, died and what is more -
Home gone, and family as well,
A fate of so many, I've heard tell.
Returned to tend to elderly 'kith and kin',
One chapter closed, another to begin.
Years later, by then quite elderly,
You came to our home, and became to me,
A source of love, inspiration, and to us all
A window of our history, all that's gone before.
You lived in my old home, long after I had gone.
You died, but memories of you linger on.
You were christened by your family 'Emily Kate'.
To me Great Aunt Kate was to be your fate.
The silver frame sits on my mantle shelf.
Within this frame a portrait of yourself.

Jean Rosemary Regan

Living In The Mystery

Happy days of childhood when the heart was young and free,
Looking forward all the time with child's simplicity.
Everything held promise and the hours seemed so long
Waiting with expectancy to sing life's wondrous song!
So much to discover - so much to explore,
Eager to be moving through the ever open door.
Self was all important and there was no time to spare
For stopping to extend a hand to show someone we care!

Later, with maturity life sings a different song,
Experience shows that halcyon days do not seem so long.
Often there's no time to do the things that hearts desire,
For slowing down the body lacks its once consuming fire,
Priorities are different - life has taught reserve,
Ambitions lose importance 'neath the truth of Holy Word!
There's more time for others, time to stop and be aware
Seeing hidden beauty that we did not know was there.
Acknowledging dependence on the One who meets life's need,
Living in the fullness of His mercy and His creed,
Each day being cherished, whatever age is known,
Remembering each one is a gift from Him upon the Throne!
To use it for His purposes until our heart can know
True peace, and love's contentment to share where're we go.
Each age in life is relevant to learn the truth of living
In the wonder and the mystery of God's almighty giving.

Elizabeth Bruce

I Remember When . . .

I remember when it was hard to forget
My fluttering heart;
The smile gripping my face;
And my soaring, weight-less soul,
When I gazed into his eyes.
I remember when it was hard to forget
How my skin would burn
As if singed by a star sent from the Heavens above
Whenever he touched me tenderly.
I remember when it was hard to forget
The caustic tears;
The infinite love and adoration;
And how I was hypnotised by his longing gaze
Whenever he told me he loved me.
I remember when it was hard to forget
That I was so in love; I couldn't imagine
A life without him.
I remember when it was hard to forget
My first true love.

Jessica Wallace

Nine Or Maybe Ten

When I was a kid
We used to have a scream
Looking back on those days
It seems, as if it were a dream.

For the kids today
Are in a different time
Their outlook on life
Is totally different to mine.

Although the money
In those days we had not
We treasured our laughter
And the things, that we'd got.

For today money is nothing
Phones and computers are in place
Kids keeping up with others
It's just a (rat race).

Buy something today
Tomorrow it's out of date
And when I was a kid
It would be safe to stop out late.

I'm sorry to say
The world was better then
When I was a youngster
Of nine or maybe ten.

Rob Passmore

THE SWEET SHOP LONG AGO

When I taste chocolate on my tongue,
It takes me back to when I was young,
Then I was just a small boy,
Then it was my pride and joy,
To go to the corner sweet shop and spend sixpence,
The jars on display seemed so immense,
And my pleasure was intense,
To see the sweetie jars all array,
Sixpence in those days seemed to go a long way,
I could pick and choose all day,
You went through a latticed door,
And kicked the sawdust off the floor,
The owner was a Mrs Jones,
She used to have an ear trumpet,
And it was tuppence for a crumpet,
Tuppence too, for liquorice sticks,
And for various pick and mix,
Or you could get a bag of toffee,
Or creams that tasted lovingly of coffee,
Mint humbugs, acid drops,
Chewing gum, gob stops,
Fizzy sweets that went ker-plop,
You would give Mrs Jones your money,
And, if she was feeling particularly sunny,
She would give you a free comfit that tasted of honey
But if I was especially good,
Done all my chores and hadn't been rude,
Mum would say, 'You haven't been tempting fate'
'And you've eaten all the greens off your dinner plate,'
'I'm going to treat you to a bar of chocolate,'
She would dress up in her new hat,
And I'd be grinning like the Cheshire cat,

Round the corner we'd go together,
And Mum and Mrs Jones would blether,
While I could choose my favourite chocolate,
Then home again I couldn't wait,
I would give Mum a goodnight kiss,
Then to my chocolate, oh what bliss!
I often think back to those days long ago,
When time ticked ever so slow,
Then sweet shops were really shops,
Owned by numerous Mrs Jones,
But now their day is gone.

Alan Pow

MY MOTHER

My mother was full of thought-provoking quotes
Which fitted any and every situation;
Words from the Bible or Shakespeare, such as those,
Always aptly suitable for the occasion.

One such quote, though from where I cannot say
Was 'a cock stride a day' I remember,
Describing the extra minutes of daylight each day
After the shortest dark day in December.

And those extra minutes led to long sunny days
And lovely evenings when in the garden we'd sit;
I remember my mother in so many special ways
But those evenings are one of my favourite.

My mother and father were both quite strict
Though love always tempered the discipline.
My brothers and I, I recall, oft got the stick!
But it was a house full of love with my kin.

In her time I'd say mother was very well learned.
'She should go to the Grammar,' her teacher said,
But apprisal of this to her parents only earned
'Out of the question' and she was sent of to bed!

And now, quotes and all, she's gone, we are apart
And memories of her all that's left to suffice,
But until we meet again she'll never leave my heart;
She was the jewel in the crown, a pearl of great price.

Marlene Allen

Pictures

The picture's getting yellow,
It was so long ago,
People in the frame,
Stay with a youthful glow,
Trapped behind the glass,
Forever in the pose,
The only thing that fades,
Are the petals on the rose.

W Curran

THE DARK SAD DAY

It creeps by slowly
  When we are young,
The time we want
  Will never not come,
But when we are old
  The years fly by before begun.

And in that flight
  You find, old friends
Do one by one
Like old soldiers - fade away,
  To leave you alone
To face the dark sad day.

H E Hayward

My Dad

What can I say about my dad
He is my friend
He is the one
Who has taught me right from wrong

But wrong, no there is no wrong
Just the right to choose
To stand and say
I am what I am

He's given me knowledge
He's given me hope
He's given me strength
To stand alone

There's much more that I could say
But to the person that I respect
I would have to say thank you,
Thank you for being *my* dad!

Janet Potter

A GREAT HOBBY

It's four in the morning I'm up with the lark
Going fishing with a friend even though still dark
We load up the car, then it's off to the sea
My friend, all our tackle, my dog and me
We arrive at the coast so tranquil and calm
I just can't wait to try out my arm
All tackled up casting out my six ounce lead
Enjoying our fishing whilst others still in bed
Watching my rod, was that a little nod
Striking hard I wonder is it a dab or a cod
Pumping up and down, need to get that line in
Adrenaline flowing what a way to begin
Slowly but surely it comes through the water
I hear my friend shout what on earth have you caught
Running into the surf, slipping his hand into its gill
It's a bloody big cod he was heard to shrill
Just a few more fish we took from the sea
Thinking all we need now are some chips for our tea
Driving home, chatting you could hear us say
The fishing was great and we've had a great day

Dave Ireland

DAYS GONE BY

I remember
when we were children
happy running round
free of any care or woe,
how my mother used to say
'I remember twenty years ago . . .'
Time has passed
and we are grown
but suddenly I'm saying
'I remember twenty years ago . . .'
And then I laugh
think of Mum with love,
and smile,
knowing all the while
she is watching me and laughing
as I do what every generation
is compelled to do -
- compare the old with the new!

Wendy Ray

Sarah And The Garden

I remember when Dad had a garden in 1936
He grew chrysanthemums in pots on tall, round sticks,
With delicate, curly, petal heads on deeply coloured leaves,
Some in a glasshouse, some near trees.

I remember Sarah wiping away her tears,
Living in an orphanage where no one hears.
Matron's birthday, she said, would pass without her gift.
Grandma had forgotten and was inclined to drift.

Now Dad had a garden, didn't I say?
It didn't take long to persuade him to give one away
And when, later on, we came out of school
He stood holding the plant in the lamp lit pool.
A beautiful mauve, all dewy and bright
Surprised little Sarah a lovely sight.

We watched as she carried it to the door
The warmth I felt then at what I saw and
The picture of Matron calling 'Please come in'
Fills my memories to the brim,
For I joined in her party and stayed to tea
And the joy of Dad's garden passed on to me.

Pauline Burton

I Remember It Well

My memory is quite unique
It goes back to childhood days
As it is almost photographic
I roll it back, in colour, like a play.

Life in the country was wonderful
A barefoot child among the clover
Sent to the city to go to school
The halcyon days were sadly over.

When a living I had to earn
Dressmaking was the trade I chose
But in the war one had to learn
That other jobs were of more use.

I married my soldier in forty-three
Next year our baby was born
He never returned, it was left to me
To bring up the child on my own.

Working hard for many a year
Before I became another man's wife
Dressmaking turned into a teaching career
Which provided a new start in life.

A widow now, long since retired
Of four great grandchildren I can boast
My long memory is unimpaired
But I forget I've put on the toast.

Lisa Wolfe

One Of Those Days

Well I think it's going to be one of those days,
You know those days that drag on forever,
When nothing seems to fall into place,
And nothing fits together.

Oh, why can't it be one of those days,
Remember those days of long ago,
When life didn't seem like a race,
Oh, where did those days go?

Well I know it could be one of those days,
It's really up to me,
Not what I do, or what I say,
It's just simply the way I see.

Yes, I think it's going to be one of those days,
You know those days you wish would last forever,
When everything seems to fall into place,
And everything fits together.

Kieran Brogan

I Remember (Anna's Last Dance On The 2000 Day)

She did not stop just danced away
Her brother Sam was so amazed
He laughed and thought she was great
The Spice Girls song was all she heard
She danced and danced till Mummy and Daddy came
We all cuddled her and said 'Happy New Year'
Please Jesus for all of us, she must be saved
But they did not know God had plans
She was never to dance again on the 2001 day
Alas 2000 year was going to be oh so sad
For the next eight months Anna was back again
Alone behind that door, she fought and fought away
But though they tried and tried so hard
She was not to see her fourth birthday
Anna asked for her party dress of course
Horse's slippers were already bought
Pongo she also had
All she wanted to come home to see Sam
Then Jesus said come with me, there will be no more pain
Enfolded her in His arms and spirited her away
We will remember the 2001 New Year Day
I hope Jesus will allow her to dance that day
Sam was so sad he had lost his mate
But still promises to dig her up some day
We hope he will forget but just remember
How Anna danced that day.

Lorna Baker (Grandma)

Echoes Of Immortal Love

Remember not
it is I
who was gauche,
awkward and rough
through the years,
but that I love you
though I am dead.

Silent together;
we did not talk
of love or anything
through the years.
Voiceless
I love you;
love is not dead.

You did not know
my feelings.
You could not know
my thoughts of you
were fond
through the years.
Know now I am dead.

Through the years
you cried - remember?
For I was ungentle;
clumsy, inept;
selfish and blind.
Forgive me I pray
now I am dead.

I'm glad my hurt
through he years
has died.
Now tender, not cold;
sympathetic, not proud;
know that I care;
love did not die.

In the quiet think
our love
through the years
is real.
In the silence rest.
Only I died.
Love is not dead.

And in the stillness
peaceful be.
With love still
in death's still hold.
As so it was
still so it be
through eternal years.

C J Gaskin

THE FUNERAL

I came to pay my last respects
And to offer support to you
I came to show you that I care
As all good friends should do

I felt the tears rise in my soul
As I sat behind you that day
I wanted so much to come and help
But couldn't find words to say

I stood outside and watched you cry
And wanted to help if I could
But somehow I couldn't bring myself
To hug like I knew I should

You apologised as you hugged me
You said you knew you shouldn't
I would have said something comforting
But - somehow - I just couldn't

I'm sorry for your dad
I share your grief with you
And if ever you need me
I'll see what I can do.

Sarah Patterson

MOTHER

God, I remember it all so well,
The Look!
The seething!
How she loved to nurse her anger.

She'd sit on that chair
Fingernails clicking;
Always clicking!
With contempt for company.

But she's gone now,
Friends who were behind her
- Where are they?
Hiding in the shadows of yesterday.

Her voice hangs in my front room
Her laugh is lost forever.
Was it what she wanted?
Is she happy now?

I remember her coffin,
The service and the flowers,
The mourners burdened with guilt
And the eyes of the village.

Salve Regina!
Rest in peace,
The Lord is with you,
May He forgive you.

Mary Sharron Coll

For Ken

Farewell, my closest friend,
My brother, broken but alive
To all he glory in Your heavenly home.

Adieu and au revoir -
We'll meet again
In that fair land we dreamed of long ago.

Your golden hair I oft caressed
Now silver-white upon your weary brow.
Hold high the torch -
The love of God will never pass us by.

My precious Ken, come back
One radiant morn
And speak to me in accents clear.
I hear your voice amid the tumbling waves -
The skylark sings your praise.
There is no death -
But rest with those you love.

Marcella Pellow

My Childhood Memories

My father had a field behind our house,
In it he kept a few hens and two cows,
Nearby we had a recreation park,
Where sometimes we'd play all day until dark,
It didn't have much, only four swings were in it,
But we would play football, rounders and cricket.
Behind was a wood with trees large and small,
My friend climbed one once, then had a bad fall,
We all ran for help to a nearby farm,
Then we discovered she had a broken arm.
Sometimes in the summer we would frolic and play
And hide from each other amongst the hay.
Sometimes we would sit and read a book,
Or go for a paddle down in the brook.
Then of course I love to remember
The bonfire and fireworks every November.
Then there followed the joy of Christmas Day,
To me that was perfect in every way.
We would hang up our stocking on the big mantleshelf,
Lie awake in our beds watching for Santa himself.
In the morning we awoke to presents galore,
Books, toys and games; who could ask for more!
After Christmas came the frost and snow,
We would slide or toboggan and snowballs we'd throw.
When the weather was too bad to go out and play
We would curl up by the fire, indoors we would stay
In the bosom of the family all cosy and warm,
We knew we were safe and would come to no harm.

Muriel Read

SWEETHEART

There once was a boy by the name of Chris,
Each moment spent with him was just pure bliss,
As time went by our friendship grew,
I promised to him I would be true.

He would chase me, this boy named Chris,
And when he caught me, he'd steal a kiss,
You might think his behaviour was quite bold,
But we were only five years old.

Came the day the family moved away,
And no more with my sweetheart did I play,
Did I forget those days of bliss?
Well, I gave my baby boy the name of Chris!

Pauline Wilkins

I Remember

I remember years ago when I was a lad
I was a devil undipped I was really bad.
I caused my mother so much grief and pain
I remember shoes that did let in the rain.
I remember the war years when I was a child
When the bombs were dropping we would all go wild.
I remember rationing bread pudding every day
'Eat it up' Mam would say 'or there will be hell to pay.'
Camphorated oil we had rubbed on our chests
It was so smelly and it stained all our vests.
Then there was bitter quinine so horrible to take
Mother had to take some first just for our sakes.
Boils we had all over mine were very bad
Yet they were happy days when I was a lad.
We would make model boats out of wood and of tin
We would disappear for the day and they'd wonder where we'd been.
We could wander through the woods and never ever come to harm
Nowadays if kids are missing for five minutes their parents are alarmed.

Don Goodwin

I Remember When

Christmas Eve would find us kids
Tucked up in our beds
Three excited children
Wondering what presents would they get

The loud knock at the door
In a voice so very deep
We heard Father Christmas say
Are your children sound asleep?

Heavy feet upon the stairs
We hid under the sheets
Santa shone his torch on us
But we pretended to be asleep

Three stockings hung on our beds
Had Santa really gone?
No he lives with us all year long
For as we grew and years moved on
Well what a great surprise
Santa wasn't Santa
But Mum with Dad's boots on

G Morrisey

The Garden

I remember a small garden
Long ago
With sunshine flowers or
Shining snow

The tall tree in the corner stood
Long ago
With fireworks sometimes
Or friendly shadow

Our dog used times
Long ago
To search and play and time
Never varied in this quiet spot

And now many years ahead
Long ago
Can mark the spot of where
I stood times, a time then forever long ago.

John Amsden

I Remember

I see a tiny cottage, with others in a row
Set beside a railway line as trains went to and fro
The cottage door was open, old time pictures were in view
Emotion overcame me, for it was someone that I knew!

She was standing by the griddle, tell tale lines upon her face
Bustling here and there, like she was in a race
Sweet aroma of golden bread filled the air
I remember, she used to be so fair, so fair

It was like she turned and saw me, not possible I knew
I was jolted out of daydream, as the train's long whistle blew
Shall I run to her? Will she know I'm there
Will I put my arms around her tell her that I care?

Back in reality, warm and cosy felt I
What does it matter? thought I, as I gave a little sigh
To have these treasured memories mean everything to me
Yes I remember, she was my grandma, you see!

E Corr

LOOKING BACK

I cannot quite remember when, I did not remember then.
When did I first start to reminisce, on sad times and of happiness?
Perhaps my young children gave a willing ear, to memories that I hold dear.
As they grow they are so sure, of how those same tales can be a bore.
Sometimes we lose some of that veneration, we expect from that next generation.
They don't want to hear the ways, we did things in the olden days.
Their days will come, they'll get the blame and bore their children just the same.
This habit now holds nothing new, for that is what the old folk do.

T A Napper

RECOLLECTIONS

Flames flickering, making shadows on the wall.
Families gathered together, not quite all.
Thoughts gathering to others not present this year,
Loving messages going far and near.
Carols resounding in the air, Dad sat proudly on the organ stool.
Mum on the piano, adding her part.
How it gladdens the heart to remember,
To realise today is the greatest birthday ever.
Jesus my Saviour came as a babe,
Came to save a lost race, praise His name, ever the same.
Born in a manger, no room in the Inn,
For the precious Son of God, who died to take away our sin.
What a wonderful day, how I pray I will always remember this
Wonderful birth, Jesus came to this earth, for you and for me.
He came to redeem all persons on earth.
But as at His birth, there was no room, so now 2000 years later
for many there is no room for Jesus.
Millions ignore His birth, to their peril.
Thank God for parents who showed us the way, to perfect redemption
To love, joy and peace, which will never cease.
Thank God for all who helped on the way.
To show us the light to eternal day.

Phyllis D Friend

Who?

Someone I know said you look well
She knew darn well I've been through hell
I said you don't like what you see
Full of 'life' and 'fantasies'
She will retaliate
Which direction will she take?
Pretends she doesn't see me there
'But' if we told the truth
We are so alike we could be twins
Often we take off on 'wings'
Soon we will reach 'maturity'
Like every other living soul
Each side of life we have to know
So do as others feel your way
You are like any other girl or boy
To chuck away your baby toys

Edna Knight-Jones

Absent

At the end of the ward
a cross upon the wall,
when one is dead,
they remake the bed,
no trace
of one at all.

Bernadette O'Reilly

MEMORIES

My childhood days are past and gone
But with sweet memories they linger on.
Swimming in the river that flowed through fields,
Sitting on a river bank eating a picnic meal.
Meeting friends, playing games
Calling out each other's names.
Waiting for my boyfriend to call
To take me dancing, at the village hall.
Church on Sundays, then taking a stroll
In the warm summer evenings
Before the months turned cold.
These memories are with me
When I sit in my room alone,
Of village life, and tales that were told,
Oh those happy days of long long ago.

Rosemary Gill

WARTIME MEMORIES

I was just thirteen at the start of the war,
I thought at first it was just a bore.
1942 brought it home to me,
My cousin was shot down over Germany.
Rationing had started we all had our book,
We often wondered what we could cook.
Tenpen'th of meat didn't go far,
And there was no petrol for running the car.
Blackouts were in, shouts of put out that light,
Wail of the sirens day and night.
The sight of the men coming home again,
Most of them wounded suffering from pain.
Entertaining the troops was the done thing,
Keeping up their moral was everything.
The bombing of cities was very sad,
It made us thought of what we had.
1944 came and I was wed,
The war would end soon everyone said.
Food was short we had to make do,
Mashed parsnip for cream on a trifle for two.
We learned many ways to do our bit,
Socks for the forces we used to knit.
One night a bomb dropped very near,
Under the stairs we trembled in fear.
They were after the aerodrome not far away,
I've never forgot it to this day.
At the end of the war everyone sang,
Hooters went and church bells rang.
The girls and boys came home at last,
To live free once more and forget the past.

Then news of the atrocities came to light,
The death of people just couldn't be right.
Where is our God I heard people say,
We could only get down on our knees to pray
That this terrible war never happens again,
And that all who were killed didn't die in vain.

A Stapleton

Memorial

I feel the earth warm and dry,
It's part of me from the ground to the sky.

I have lived and died this tomb of earth,
A memorial for what it's worth,

The coals are cold, my ashes old,
This house of the dead, this is the bed of mortal remains,
I go ever on not just in lyrics and songs,

A king of old, my soul arose in smoky flames,
Souls are reborn in the new dawn,
But the barrows to remind, a king is gone,

I rise again in songs of old,
Earth, wind and fire, nature only desire,
This is the life we all acquire,
Nature the real desire.

K M Clemo

THE VOICE

Dusk was stealing over the sea . . .
Waves were rolling, rolling to me.
Dark clouds were gathering in the sky
Night was coming by and by.
As the wind rose high, across the sea a faint sound
Came like someone calling me.
The tall reeds caught the sound and whispered
It among themselves.
Waves tossed over rocks and roared along the shore.
Then the voice across the sea began to sing
It sang a song which I had once loved best of all.
The waves rolled to the tune and the reeds repeated the words.
As I listened to that lovely song, with it came
The wonderful memory of long lost yesterdays.
Dusk now turned to darkness, the moon came out with
her sad pale light.
As the voice across the sea called the past days to me
I wished I could go back to those days so long ago
And do again the things I did then . . . now only memories.
Most of all I remembered the owner of the voice across the sea.
All was quiet as I walked away, the waves were splashing gently
Over the rocks and I knew that never again
Would I forget that song . . . or the voice across the sea.
That voice once . . . so well known to me.

Jennifer M Trodd

Christmas When I Was A Child

Christmas was great when I was a child
All the family came round, unwrapped presents, went wild
On Christmas day Mum cooked the food
The next day we went to uncle's, who was in a good mood
My uncle got a turkey, a really big bird
We ate it in earnest thanked auntie for the expense it incurred
At New Year Gran came up on top
She roasted gammon which was the pick of the crop
I missed it now I'm grown up and alone
Many of these people have died or moved on
I hope one day to have Xmas cheer
If I have kids we'll go mad each year!

P Edwards

Memories

In our residential home
There are no doubt treasures galore
Beloved by all their owners
Who keep them in all store

Old letters that were written
By the writers now dead
Books cherished in childhood
Though now they are seldom read

Bits of cracked china
More precious to some than gold
Photos that are now depicting
The young now grown old

A useless collection you may think
Of rubbish you may say
But we have not the heart
Just to throw it all away

D Sheasby

My Life

(Written from the mind of my baby boy . . . Andy!)

Things have changed and continue to change,
And sometimes it's hard to see,
That here I am just a few months old,
When back then . . . there wasn't no 'me'!

I remember things so clearly,
Yet it all seems so far away,
And there are so many things going on in my life,
All squashed up and crammed into one day.

Sometimes I think they expect too much,
Although they do say that I am bright,
Will I speak, do I crawl, can I sit, will I walk?
Well let's see - maybe I might!

I remember my journey into this world,
It wasn't so crash hot you know,
It took quite a while, just ask my mum,
Yet looking at her, it didn't really show.

I remember the day she first held me,
I do believe it made her cry,
And looking back now, I can honestly say,
I really can't remember why!

Maybe they were tears of happiness,
Or relief from just having me,
Because now our life together is great,
You only have to look at us to see!

Maria Cracknell

I REMEMBER WHEN . . . NOT FORGOTTEN

I remember the days when I was young
And the world seemed a kinder place.
Very few cars and no TV
Things moved at a gentler pace.

We walked to school and played in the fields
Carefree and full of joy.
Whips and tops and skipping ropes
Hoops and kites were our toys.

People worked hard for little return
But were ready to help and share.
When trouble beset their neighbours
And burdens too hard to bear.

I remember the day the war was declared
And families split apart.
But friendships were formed and all rallied round
Helping keep fear and gloom from the heart.

While men served their country in foreign lands
Women took on a new role.
Factories and shops, buses and farms,
Keeping the home front this was their goal.

It was not easy going but it taught one to trust
In the one who is ever near.
For the promise He gave is with me still
'I go before, never fear.'

F L Brain

CRUEL LOVE

When he was a young man
his girl jilted him.
The pain of it shattered him.
He sought solace in food,
after a while his pain eased
for food became his mistress.
As the years passed
his love grew,
his body grew,
his heart grew . . .

Much later, his mistress became viscous.
Tormenting him,
mocking him,
crippling him.
Until finally, his heart broke . . .

Valerie McKinley

A CHRISTMAS WISH

Once I had a lonely dog
who walked the streets alone.
No friendly hand to stroke me,
No home to call my own.
I wandered in the fields and towns,
in rain and wind and snow.
I scavenged for my food and drink
I had no place to go.
Another Christmas Day approaching
My body ached with pain.
I wished for someone to love me,
someone to give me a name.
Then on Christmas Eve she found me.
Her voice was gentle and sweet.
Her touch so soft and tender,
she swept me off my feet.
She named me then, her Christmas Star
and my Christmas wish came true.
She told me 'I've been waiting
for a special dog like you.'
Now when Christmas comes and goes
I pray to the gods that be
'Thank you for my happy life,
and all you've given me.
But look after all the other dogs
who live out on the street,
and send a special person
to sweep them off their feet.

Patricia Heard

SECRET CORNER

In the corner of our garden
Stood a graceful lilac tree;
I fenced it off and made a gate -
A hiding place for Me.

I put a board beside my gate,
With 'Private' written there;
I laid a piece of carpet down
And, on it, placed a chair.

There I'd sit for hours on end,
Engrossed in book or thought;
Sometimes listening to the thrush -
By his entrancing trilling, caught.

When the sky was overcast,
And then poured down the rain -
I'd run inside till the sun came out
Then hurry down again.

My spirits soared, and my heart sang
As, on the top-most bough,
My friend, the blackbird, trilled his song
For me, alone, I vow.

Was he trying to tell me
What was hidden there?
A chest of buried treasure
Beneath my little chair!

For, all the hours I had sat,
Completely unaware,
I'd been guarding Mother's secret -
A hiding place for her!

Bee Wickens

A Fighter Pilot Remembers

I cleaved the air and azure skies on broad wings not my own;
Through crystal ether, up I'd rise to vistas little known.
With god-like power at my command, I'd dive and bank and soar;
Breath-taking speeds could I demand, and make my engine roar.
No heights, it seemed, could I not try: no distance was beyond me.
Through rain and cloud did my bird fly, and brightest sunshine
found me.

As my heart sang and pulses beat, I sought for heaven's portals.
Here, surely, I should angels meet and parley with Immortals!
Nay, here was no Elysian scene: no blessed, holy rapture;
But hell-fire, rather, swift and keen, bringing death or capture.
In sky, pellucid-blue and arched, no god-like forms I'd meet:
Only hostiles skyward marched on cruel Aeolian feet.

This bird I flew, in sun and cloud, death-spitting songs she'd sing me.
Her voice - staccato, harsh and loud - cacophony did bring me.
And so, instead of peace and light, we'd twist and turn and rise;
With demons rather did we fight until we'd cleared the skies.
But fly we did, and sing and spit, and when the sky was clear,
Then in our nest alert we'd sit, till new foes ventured near.

On this bright day, now peace abides, when I am so light-hearted,
The pure, sweet air for joy she rides: all hostiles have departed.
No longer need we watch the sun for fiery fierce attack;
Nor cry, 'Red Two, keep both eyes peeled! For God's sake,
watch my back!'
Through banks of cloud, or misty air, or purest azure skies,
All unmolested - free, secure - see my bird heav'nwards rise!

Ivor Haythorne

Christmas

Must I think of Christmas?
Must I think of you?
Do you remember long ago
When love for us was new?

Those happy days together
With all our friends around.
That lovely, lovely Christmas
When true love we had found.

And now I think of Christmas
With a sorrow I can't bear
Why did you cease to love me?
Why did you cease to care?

I do not know the answer
I really loved you so.
Did you leave me for another?
Is that why you had to go?

M Barber

Remember Me

Remember me,
I was the one that played the games when no one else
Would come around.
I was the dead cowboy on the floor, Lone Ranger's partner
Or the customer at the door.

Remember me,
I was the one that made castles with your pillows,
And wrapped those warm sturdy walls around you
At night so you would drift into your land of make believe
With your protective armour shining bright.

Remember me,
I am the one that wiped away those tears,
I'd sit you upon my knee and wrap my arms around you tight
Until you felt safe enough to smile and throw away the fears.

Remember me,
I'm the one that held all your insecurities
In the palm of my hand and sorted them out, one by one,
Until they were all gone.

Remember me,
Well I'm still here, inside I'm still the same,
Although you can't see, now I cry the tears
I fear the pain and carry the insecurities,
How time has changed,
Please! Remember me!

Dianne Audrey Daniels

I REMEMBER 2000

I remember 2000 that golden year
Of floods, fueltax protests and the Dome
Man Utd chickening out of the FA Cup
To play the WCC in Brazil far from home

Working in a factory for £15 per week
Below the minimum wage of £3.70 per hour
Sydney Olympics where we won a pot of gold
European Championships, not our finest hour

But my greatest memory of 2000 is
Seeing my late Grandma's cremation
On 12th January in Hereford
While she passed to God's new paradise nation.

H G Griffiths

Airfix Kits

I remember buying Airfix kits
of Lancasters and Hurricanes
at Woolworths down in Leeds,
but never comprehending
how attacking and defending
were such necessary deeds.

I remember my dexterity
and waiting ever patiently
for Humbrol paint to dry,
but never realising
how defeat was agonising
in a war-infested sky.

I remember dogfights in the street
outside my fifties council house
where winning was assured,
but never contemplating
how my mind was emulating
something many souls deplored.

I remember falling from the skies
of make-believe and aeroplanes
and landing in my youth,
where I continued fighting
for the wrongs that needed righting
as I targeted the truth.

Iain W Wade

As A Book

I am always remembering
Past days a lifetime
Has disappeared gone all the years
the days of my youth
All the growing up now
Seems a dream, all the heartache and tears
I see everything clearly
As if it were yesterday
Happy times, our mum and dad
Songs of our day
Will always bring memories
And the thoughts of the good times we had
We move on the years
Bring more joy and promises
Life has its richness rewards
But the memories will stay
Of all those past days
As a book turn the pages once more

Jeanette Gaffney

REMEMBRANCE

Dreaming of a white Christmas, sparkling snow!
Fairy tales, frolic, sprinkled trees, dappled lights,
Oh! Those faint remembered days of 'long ago'
Our winters now so wet and muddy,
Dark, drear, flu-ridden, called 'earth warming'!
Someone must be joking, we are frozen to the bone,
Trying to cheer asking children, scooting snowballs,
Friendly fights a laugh, a shout 'I'll get you.'
As we ducked, bobbed, scooping snowballs, aiming fast,
No scolding on being hit, cold water not same reaction,
Mighty snowmen built with gusto, carrot for his snout,
Old hat atop, button eyes agrinning, ribbon mouth,
Benignly watching waving heels, from toboggans flying,
Digging in too deep on snowy surfaced slopes,
Snow and kindergartens do not go hand in hand!
As we slide here and there on pond or shore,
Full of joy in our winter woollies, covered ears,
'You lucky blighters!' laugh our kids, 'Those days!'
'Not really bad,' our wise reply,
'Too much traffic now you know,' when
Lo and behold, 2000 Christmas came in white
'Never do to lose out upon the millennium,'
Whispered the weather man, with a wink,
As in joyous hope we ring in,
The chimes to 2001 celebrations,
Secure in Christmas eternal story white or not,
'I Jesus came to guide you, no matter what the season,'
God's love for man, beyond our human comprehension!

Anne Mary McMullan

In Their Place

In my youth, I shared
Many a friendship,
- With those -
Of whom, I'd have given a fortune,
To have been in their place.

But now time has marched on,
And the years of life, have chosen,
Changes of position to make,
And though they're still the same people,
Worthy of anyone's company to grace.

They're now forever parted,
And the love, that they once shared for each other,
- No longer in their lives,
- Still owns a place.

And that, of which I once desired,
And would have given so much for,
- Has sadly -
Been lost, without trace.

Bakewell Burt

This Locket

Open up the locket.
See the photos there inside.
That's Grandad and Grandma,
Long before she died.

It's just a little trinket
She wore it everyday,
Until she got a gold one,
By then, she'd long turned grey.

When she came in, she showed me,
With eyes so starry bright,
We danced around the kitchen
And I shared in her delight.

For at its heart, block perfume,
She could touch behind her ears,
A place then there for pictures
The same it now still bears.

I remember how she patted it,
Satisfied, content.
She'd scrimped and saved, felt guilty
But her money was well spent.

I know you loved your grandma,
The trinket came to me.
You can have it, with the story,
Worth more than gold you see.

I was just a little girl
And it's all so long ago
But my mother's joy that day
It set my heart aglow.

Pauline Boncey

Golden Age Of Steam

I remember when . . .
steam trains raced across patchwork countryside,
neat fields bordered by brush or fence.
Rhythmic clickety clack,
a comforting sound from beneath,
in chorus with the chuffing of the engine
puffing white clouds
into open sky.
I can still smell
the masculine scent
of carriage interiors,
of leather arm rests
and velvet-pile seats.
And hear the crispness
of the slamming doors.
No words can fully describe these things,
they are memories from
the innocence of my youth,
when such magical trips
were a yearned for respite
from a black and white existence.
Hardships were plenty,
yet people made do,
appreciating the joy
in the most simple of pleasures.
Ah yes,
I remember the
Glorious Age of Steam

Rose Dempsey

I Remember

I remember, I remember,
How it used to be,
Doors and windows left unlocked,
No fear of burglary.

I remember, I remember,
The tanner and the bob,
The farthing and the ha'penny,
And the Boy Scouts' 'bob a job.'

I remember, I remember,
I remember when
A made-to-measure three-piece suit
Would cost just two pounds ten.

I remember, I remember,
I remember then,
A pack of Woodbine cigarettes,
Was four old pence for ten.

I remember, I remember,
I remember how
We roasted chestnuts round the fire,
But it's all so different now.

I remember times long past,
But hear my tale of woe,
I can't remember things that happened
A day or two ago.

Ron Green

SKYE BRIDGE

Speed, grimy bus belching diesel and smoke,
Over the bridge to Skye.
Carry the bags of a silly old bloke
Across the island that died!

Loud the wind blows
As over I go.
Exhaust fumes fill the air,
The bridge is awash,
Whisky is tossed
To drown all the sorrows we share!

Speed, grimy bus belching diesel and smoke
Over the bridge to Skye.
Banish our care, romantics despair,
History and memories must die!

Robert Neill

FALLING RAIN

Sitting here
Listening to the rain,
Remembering the rainy days
I spent with you
The way you held me close,
To share your warmth
While it was
Pouring mercilessly with rain,
A prophecy of the tears
I would shed for you,
But in those days
The lightning lit up the sky
Like a proclamation of our love,
The thunder echoed
The beatings of our hearts,
Gale force winds
As strong as our rising emotions,
The stormy weather
Leaving damage in its wake,
Just like our love.

Farrah Mahmood

The Old Days In The Past

We met, we married a long time ago,
We worked long hours for wages so low.
No telly, no wireless, no bath; times were hard.
Just a cold tap a walk up the yard.
No holidays abroad, no carpets on floors,
But had coal on the fire; never locked doors.
Our children arrived, no pills those days.
We brought them up without state aid.
They were safe to play in the park
And old folk could walk in the dark,
There was no vallium or drugs or LSD,
We curbed our ills with a cup of tea.
If you were sick, you were treated at once
Not fill in forms and come back in six months,
No vandals, no muggings; there's nothing to do.
We were quite happy with a couple of bob.
People were happier in those far-off days,
Kinder and caring in so many ways.
Milkmen and paper-boys used to whistle and sing,
A night at the pictures was a mad fling.
We all had our share of trouble and strife
We just had to face it, that's the position of life.

Sheila Waller

I Remember When . . . Christmas Day!

I remember when I woke up
It was Christmas day
I ran downstairs excited
Pushing everything out of my way
I knew there were presents downstairs
Were there some for me?
If there were then I really wanted to see,
That was Christmas last year
Will this year be the same?
Will I get lots of presents?
Will Santa come again?
Will snow fall on Christmas Eve?
Will it snow on Christmas Day?
I really want to know
I really can't wait!

Laura Hewitt

My Sweet Belle

Oh how I loved you! My sweet Belle:
When across that bar our eyes first met;
For your warm innocent smile my heart fell.

My knees trembled under love's own spell.
I was your Romeo and you my Juliet;
Oh how I loved you! My sweet Belle.

My senses filled with your primrose smell;
And those first words you spoke - I'll never forget.
For your warm innocent smile my heart fell.

I know I promised never to kiss and tell.
But of true love with tears I've wept;
Oh how I loved you! My sweet Belle.

Two hearts true sat on love's tender shell;
Alas! From the start our fate in stone was set:
For your warm innocent smile my heart fell.

And now my darling, I wish you well;
Not one moment with you do I regret.
Oh how I loved you! My sweet Belle,
For your warm innocent smile my heart fell.

Marc Tyler

Victorian Christmas

Horses and carriages trot on snow-covered streets
Shops with bow windows displaying their treats
Ribbon-tied boxes of fondants and candies
Decorated Christmas trees and cherry liqueur brandies.

The piano in the parlour, a family sing-song
Oil-lit lanterns of an era long ago
Victorian post-boxes, seasonal greetings cards, lace-edged
Laughing children sliding their home-made sledge.

R Humphrey

Kid Covet

I would greet Christmas morning with suppressed excitement,
A day full of surprises and delightment.
Seasonal greetings I cast when all about lay snow,
A welcome warm by the fire that's kept in glow.
Our home is decorated and awash with holly,
A room of plenty where family's jolly.
Intoned carols at this pious time
This festival act I now tell in rhyme.
Although long gone my puerile years, thoughts in mind they stay,
My fondest memories are of my childhood, so it's Christmas
every day.

John P Evans

RING THOSE WEDDING BELLS

Ring those wedding bells there's magic in the air
Ring those joy bells let's have music everywhere.
Ring out those chimes and let's be merry and have no care
Let's make a night of it - ring all those bells!

Things are swinging and there's magic beneath the Moon
Bells are ringing, hear them singing our wedding tune
Hear what they are saying - we'll be together soon
Let's make a date of it - ring all those bells!

Ding-dong, ding-dong
We'll swing along forever true
Spring song, this is our love song
Spend all my life just loving you.

Wedding bells are ringing, there's music everywhere
Ring those joy bells for there's romance in the air
Ring out, ring out those bells, there's magic for us to share
Let's make a song of it - ring all those marvellous,
Magical,
Wonderful,
Ring all those bells!

Nelson Peters

Relive Old Times

Oh just to turn the clock back
to breathe the fresh, clean air,
all this modern way of life
never, ever can compare.
We had very little money,
pace of life was slow,
there was trust and understanding,
life always seemed to flow.
Such pleasure to relive old times,
to feel a certain pride,
we had job satisfaction,
time seemed always on our side.
Remembering the steam trains
more reliable it seems,
now our high speed, high tech railway
functions only in our dreams.
Life without computers
really was sublime,
now not to surf the internet
seems to be some sort of crime.
Old fashioned, yes perhaps it was,
though we always held the key,
to a wealth of hope and happiness,
yes, most of it was free.

Dorothy M Gillway

THE OLD TENEMENT

Once she held centre stage
in people's gritty lives

A four-storeyed
monolith mouthing
pleasant platitudes
to those padding
gas lit stairways

Her grunting grey
redeemed by well-
washed windows
and polished nameplates

Gave sanctuary
to hard grafting
families living
and dying behind
her stony facade

Now this empty
sulking shell hugs
memories shaped
by clattering looms
and meddling mill smoke.

James Adams

BOMBED OUT!

Morning light pierces sore, tired eyes
Emerging from their warren of the night.
Acrid smoke and brick dust attack nostrils,
No preparation for this horrific sight!
Terraced houses reduced to rubble,
Fallen masonry and debris everywhere,
Craters and timbers block their pathway,
Heavy, the overwhelming disbelief and despair!

The German bombers departed in triumph,
A direct hit scored on the dockyard below,
Perimeter houses caught in a tidal wave
Of blast, fallen like tilting dominoes.
Their tenement flat sliced down the middle,
Furniture, belongings spilled into the street,
Yesterday, her spring-cleaning was completed,
Today, her world, shattered, lays at her feet.

The child fearfully clutches her mother's hand,
Her baby brother still asleep in the safety of arms,
The father departed by his call to war,
No longer a shield to keep them from harm.
Sudden remembrance of a world apart,
An idyllic Somerset village of holidays,
A cottage owned by a widowed aunt,
Pack a few possessions and get right away.

Queues at the station, tickets are purchased,
Pushed into carriages, already crammed,
Farewell to the city smouldering in ruins,
Depart bravely to a promised land.

Pat Heppel

MEMORIES

Here I sit in the gloom.
Look around my room,
So many memories there,
Clowns, toys, teddy bears
Collected over the years.
Some bring smiles,
Some bring tears.
Looking round my life I see
What does this tell me.
Times of joy, times of woe,
It was sad to see them go,
But that is life
They go their way,
I am here to stay.
I have precious memories to keep,
Though sometimes they make me weep,
Then the phone rings,
'Hi Mum, we're dropping round.'
Suddenly the room's alive,
Tears now gone, replaced by smiles
With them all here again,
I come alive.

P Perry

BEACON'S HILL

When you were a boy and I a girl
and summer days were warm and still,
we roamed the fields without a care
on yesterday's Beacon's Hill.

Anemones split their moonlit silver
dipping their fingers in holy rill,
buttercups threw gold sunshine
along lines on Beacon's Hill.

Fluffy clouds were drifting slow,
their reflections caress window sill,
whispering breeze in silver grass
stirred our hair on Beacon's Hill.

But time my love has passed us by,
summer jaunts into winter's chill,
can you recall those magical times
we spent kissing on Beacon's Hill?

T Webster

Reviving 45's In The Jukebox

Jukeboxes were dumped outside coffee bars, when those
Teenage haunts closed. No more love songs for a shilling
Dropped in a slot; but that's how this fickle world goes.
The Seventies dawned. With-it youths were less willing
To fumble in pockets for 'tanners' to press keys,
Or look down the list, while their fellows were milling
Around, more impatient per minute. Such cheap sprees
Could never match high delights of a pop concert.
Thus gigs represented the new decade's esprit.
Song words of Roy Orbison's 'It's Over' subvert
Recoveries of boys, to whom love brought real gloom.
But there were few records that didn't cause such hurt.
The vision of jukeboxes is an auction room
Evokes escapades we can blame on the Baby Boom.

Gillian Fisher

Such A Rare Combination

Saw her coming from the clinic; talked, exchanged phone numbers.

A phone call, date sealed; and what a date!
Eight, on a Sunday morning,
But I wasn't about to let slip chance of a lifetime;
Date with an angel.

Sunday early bird, off to purchase Sunday Mail.
On my way back was a confusion of hope and anxiety;
A gnawing feeling, would never see her.

When I saw this glorious looking lady,
It never crossed my mind,
She could be the one;
Fine head of hair, misty sweet eyes, lovely face.
Cream silk blouse, grey tweed skirt, cute black suede shoes.

I was about to walk past,
When a sing-song voice stopped me in my tracks;
How about the date?

As I escorted her to the bus terminus,
A white sports car with a young couple,
Came from behind us and slowed down;
A look of sweet confusion on the faces.

In my mind;
They must be thinking,
How can such a simple guy,
T-shirt, track bottom, trainers,
Have won the heart of this class lady?

I must say, an eternal proud secret smile, was born in my heart.
She possessed such a rare combination;
Consummate beauty, and fresh innocence.

Each time I remember the occasion;
I feel, it was a glimpse, of Heaven's splendour.

Rowland Warambwa

FATHER PRAYED

I remember when my father prayed;
Easily call back the words he often said;
Keep them in safety on the way to school,
The lessons, interval and journey back.'
And then his final words, 'Bless those we love,
All who love us,' then hard for the childish minds,
'All those for whom to pray, our duty binds.'
Thus kings or queens, MPs and rulers all,
Our councils, all those on whom a governing power may fall.
Thus day by day, my father talked with God,
For home and family, all who served abroad,
Many by name and some he had not met,
Remembered in those prayers I can't forget.

A Livings

A Small Life Taken

Let me teach you how to hold in your hand
the soul of one so young and a life so grand,
Look into your heart and try to understand
The meaning of the wishes that are planned,
then go forth with love in your heart
for 'twas you that did this life to start,
Take the time and love to play your part
look upon that little face so pert,
For in your heart you know that the time will come
when for this soul to sweet sleep it will succumb,
Not tears shed, or sorrow show, for 'tis destiny for some,
for 'tis He that has called this child to His home,
Though your love was given only weeks not years
that one small moment in time His grace shares,
Knowing of His plan helps dispel all one's fears
let me help you hold in your hand His tears.

John Clarke

INFORMATION

We hope you have enjoyed reading this book - and that you will continue to enjoy it in the coming years.

If you like reading and writing poetry drop us a line, or give us a call, and we'll send you a free information pack.

Write to :-

Triumph House Information
Remus House
Coltsfoot Drive
Peterborough
PE2 9JX
(01733) 898102